S0-BEZ-872

AS WHEN, IN SEASON

AS WHEN, IN SEASON

POEMS

[signature: Jim Schley]

JIM SCHLEY

[handwritten inscription:] For Avery: Let us continue the conversation we began? I count on that! April 2015 Jim

MARICK PRESS

Copyright © 2008 by Jim Schley

Editor: Ilya Kaminsky
Text and cover design: Ann Aspell

No part of this book may be reproduced without written permission of the publisher.
Please direct inquiries to:

Managing Editor / Marick Press / Post Office Box 36253 / Grosse Pointe Farms, Michigan 48236

Library of Congress Catalogue in Publication Data available upon request.
Schley, Jim, 1956–
As When, In Season : poems / by Jim Schley. — 1st edition.
p. cm.

ISBN 10: 1-934851-00-0
ISBN 13: 978-1-934851-00-5

FIRST EDITION

COVER AND FRONTISPIECE ART:

Segments of sculptures by Andrea Stix Wasserman, part of "Maple, Apple, Birch," an installation
created in 2001 with Elizabeth Billings for the Burlington International Airport, Burlington,
Vermont. Photographs by John Douglas. Used by permission of the artist
(www.andreawasserman.com).

SOURCES FOR EPIGRAPHS:

Bob Dylan, from "Like a Rolling Stone," copyright © 1965; renewed 1993 Special Rider Music.
All rights reserved. International copyright secured. Reprinted by permission. "The Lone
Shieling," refrain from a song often attributed to John Galt (1779–1839) or to an elusive, rueful
Anonymous. John Milton (1608–1674), from the invocation in Book I of *Paradise Lost*. Adrienne
Rich, from "Mother and Son, Woman and Man," in *Of Woman Born: Motherhood as Experience and
Institution*. Copyright ©1986, 1976 by W. W. Norton & Company, Inc. Used by permission of the
author and W. W. Norton & Company, Inc. Simone Weil, from "Réflexions sur le bon usage des
études scolaires en vue de l'amour de Dieu" in *Attente de Dieu* (Éditions Fayard, 1966): "S'il y a
vraiment désir, si l'objet du désir est vraiment la lumière, le désir de lumière produit la lumière."
Elizabeth Bishop, from "Crusoe in England" in *The Complete Poems: 1927–1979* (Farrar Straus and
Giroux, 1984). Used by permission of the publisher. Arthur Schopenhauer (1788–1860), from the
section called "Government" in the essay "Human Nature." Czeslaw Milosz, the section called
"Longing" from the poem "Notes" in *New and Collected Poems: 1931–2001* (Ecco, 2003).
Copyright © 1988, 1991, 1995, 2001 by Czeslaw Milosz Royalties, Inc. All rights reserved.

Small Press Distribuition
(800) 869–7553 / spd@spdbooks.org

Wayne State University Press
(800) 978-732

Printed in Canada

CONTENTS

DWELLING

IN SEASON

BORNE OUT

How does it feel
To be on your own
With no direction home

Bob Dylan

Fair these broad meads —
These hoary woods are grand —
But we are exiles from our fathers' land.

"The Lone Shieling"

THE LAST SUMMER

Sunrise erupted on a cloud-ridged horizon.
Land so level, sloping just inches from the lake.
Hear the squeak of oars, the slap and swivel
half in darkness, edging shoals as the boat
came clear to open water. I would hold
a tin of worms in warm dirt. My granddad,
sturdy and terse, would ferret them out
with a pocket knife, then quarter an apple
to stall our hunger. Hours until breakfast,
the boat wandered on faint waves, un-anchored.
The man would smoke, or with several strokes
nudge us in among reeds to a sinkhole.
In one of his moods, with little to say

as bobbers ticked on the wavering glare.

Land Alone

Some cartographer's error
and we squandered days,
a river on the map now swamp:
glacial fissures drained to marsh,
so a channel angled south goes east then north,
to halt canoes at a beavers' dam, trunks big as cabin logs.
Millions of droplets per cubic inch, and brief efflorescence
in stalks, leaves and lacy ferns already by August
curling for an onslaught of snow. Head-high grass
spread by prows keeps no trail of keel, paddle blade, or feet
as flies toil and bite, as boots spew rot from muddy sockets.
Redwings creak on cattails like farcical guides.
Bullfrogs thrum directions only a blackbird could decipher.
Who are you to the herons, to the beavers felling trees?
Who cares for you? say the barred owls,
as soft to disappear as puffs of mist.
How far to your vanishing point?

Our lives became things,
callused joints and scarlet knees,
with hair tied back to tumble behind. Six of us,
strangers since, a rank and cantankerous crew:
On day three we crossed a flowage in porridge-thick fog,
tracking island to island by compass
with twelve-foot visibility encircling each boat.
Near noon a bush plane, then growling saws.
The village on Red Lake. But remember

how the land made its own way, with no one there.

War Zone

Cacophonous rooster and mewling calves, as shod hooves
clack on stones. In the courtyard of a half-built manor house,
moonlight pries among shouldering weeds, beaming clean
and clear into window gaps, the missing roof open wide to
the rearranged stars of a southern sky through clouds wan as
dried flax. Down the hill I hear songs, cowbells, and to the east,
beyond the nearest rim of hills, spread along the broad basin
of a dusty lake, there's Managua — miles of sheds and acres of
rubble from quakes or combat, the streets patrolled by battle-
worn school kids. City of half a million that barely casts a glow.

·

Oil smoke, and the rubbery stench of garbage fires in door-
yards. All is dust, dry as chalk with drought. When we stumble
off our bus in Ocotal, children flutter and light, reaching for
binoculars and cameras. Their parents stand back — they
know what we've paid for. We walk to the square, find a
bench in shade by the candy-striped pole of a barbershop
whose *jefe* appears, brandishing shears. He grumbles, winks,
then pantomimes clipping my shaggy head. The crowd jostles
close to see what I'll do. Low mountains, no taller than New
England's, but furry with heat. I smile, slow and blank, then
stand, trying to raise my threadbare Spanish like a little flag. All
at once there's gunfire, three quick bursts, metal chewing metal,
and though they call out, I don't know what they say. I run for
the bus.

·

In the plaza it's cooler. The day, hot as inside an engine but
abruptly there was lighting and finally rain. Alongside a soldier
— we couldn't speak for thunder-crash and lack of common
words but we shouted, laughed, and slapped each other's
backs, wet shirts smacking brightly. Quiet at last, the evening
briefly unclenches. And the ground feels solid after yesterday's
earthquake; I woke to someone yelling *Doorways are strongest!*

so we jammed together at the threshold as that floor surged
and sank, gelatinous as our heaving intestines. Gazing now into
night, there's booming and ringing, completely ambiguous. I
step blindly, crossing between sporadic streetlights along stacked
barrels of treetrunks with spiky skin and fronds like the shredded
spears I remember waving as a child on Palm Sunday.

·

In the road below: thin man propped on the curb with a
gun in his lap, hat pulled down siesta-style. Overhead, some
spreading, deciduous tree. I think I hear whistling, then I'm
sure — chuckling with talk, an invisible card game with three
or four militiamen, sitting on branches like elves in a cloud.
Hidden by leaves, but their rifles gleam. The one on the ground
tips his hat a few inches, unblinking, as the others keep chatting
though their cadence has dipped so I know they're tracking me.
I raise my hand to wave to the crouched one, to the tree above,
and walk steadily down the tilting cobbled street till their talk,
and their periodic bursts of laughter, are just vibrations in the
pendulous dark at my back.

STROKE

A lover is outside that grasp
of gravity, mother to daughter.
You hold on as I hover near.

I can't know her. There's no time.
The woman here, with tongue
fraying edges of phrases, fingertips
that fret the blanket's hem.
Smell of camphor, dust of bromide, a bed
stanchioned in perpendicular silver rods.

      You're angry: I haven't seen
the dancer she was, hot as sunlight
crisscrossed in a hand glass, elegant
and sharp. She didn't change

by shadings as in aging, but vanished
— only partly returned.
              I watch
like I'd watch someone wounded.
Yet so much of what was
is there, in your voices and hair,
the ways you both wave
at red blooms
in a glass.

HER PERIOD

Her period would arrive like a suitor
from the wider society of blood.

Awake, as dawnlight inches down
the scarred bricks above streets
that descend to the harbor from Winter Hill.

Her city at the edge of an ocean.

Through a bedside window we watched
their hide-and-seek, children scattering like seeds
then hidden in hedges like eggs.

Her gaze, no more real to me now
than steam from the morning's bath.

Bloodstains on the linen.

What a strange reprieve,
what a dry, compounded grief.

After All

When I'd purged
myself of need,
funneled off
desire to hold her,
even scraped
from my mind
the scent and weight
of that body on mine;
convinced any memory
was imaginary
I thought I could speak
carelessly, no hope
of more — maybe
a postcard, or
silence for months.
But still, after all
her voice will drill
through me. Today
when she called
the telephone
was carved of ice.
I know she said, no.
I heard her say, no.
Like Archilochus
who lost his shield,
I say fuck it,
I'll find another.

My Father's Whistle

On a darkened bus
on Thanksgiving, I was
thinking

"My father could whistle
like breeze coming home
through a spruce,"

the aisle lights
glinting like valves
down the length
of a black clarinet.

I was
breathing
through my teeth,
and with tilted lips

throat and mouth
released
a looped sigh

the first whistle came free

filigree in air
that remains —

On Green Dolphin Street

For hours that November I'd walk through London,
hoping to be carried off by a woman's glance,
but there instead
           in the boarding house parlor
found an old record, where you'd hear
inlaid, still to be retrieved
Cannonball, Coltrane, Bill Evans, all dead by then,
with Miles and two others, maybe Chambers and Cobb,
who played one song so wholly together
it took me
as I'd wished for but never understood.
Each of them loved
his own way, the tune itself
broken across two short sides
of a 45,
        made of parts
                like pieces of clothing
I began to wear when I stepped into view,

vest of stellar cold trumpetry,
        saxophone trousers and shoes of walking bass.
My hat would be flat, and riffle
        like drumskin around my ears.
And the bones of my hands learned to roam
        in gloves clean and bright as piano keys.

Where could I go?
Where was the place they found?
On Green Dolphin Street
I would make my heart a lamp
turned upward or down,
necessarily blue, whenever I'm
without a prayer

so finally free.
Each time I set out again, to stride
against all weariness to the end of the street,
strange airs in my throat,
the breeze beneath the birds,

the three or four skills I am sure of
    tingle in my fingers.

IN COMPASS: NINE ODES

Sing Heav'nly Muse . . .
And chiefly thou O Spirit, that dost prefer
Before all temples th'upright heart and pure,
Instruct me, for thou know'st . . .

John Milton

If I could have one wish for my own sons, it is that
they should have the courage of women.

Adrienne Rich

For Terpsichore

As a dancer I came so belatedly to dance
    I could never be sure to arrive right on time
        that instant when tempo and footfall coincide

under rippling arch of horn on a drumbeaten floor.
    Pivot yields a kick, turn, four steps advance

round left and four steps back to right. You saw
    me in Hamburg, under lights and masked,
        then sent a beguiling offer. Seeking one

with moves without the mannerisms of those
    schooled in ballet; whose gestures are clear,
        concise, and practical; if not a virtuoso,
            yet firm as a fulcrum. Less prance

than stride, and on stilts somehow more:
    covered in fabric and a Balinese mask,
        with bamboo switch and swathe of silk

I was another, entirely — nine feet tall
    and apparently not for certain female
        or male, the carved countenance

ambiguous to an audience, smooth
    as wood-grain upon my face, only lit
        through oval-shaped eye holes.
            A sensation as close to trance

as I've known, embodying elegance
    not just visual. As if formed anew
        from matter abstracter than muscled skin.
            Choreography is sculpting fibers upon tones.

Your *mise en scène* is harmonious dissonance,
    exacting agility and pliant allegiance
        to specified speed, painfully gradual

then quick as a shift of the lamps. You
          began as an ingenue, shopkeeper's girl
               summoned with early accolades to the capital,
                    to the *corps de l'Opéra* and bed of *le maître*.

I'm awed by the audacity, by the stance
          you struck — the Dance was yours to make
               or re-make, proprieties be damned.

Turning aside without flounce and pirouette
          from an orderly Swiss future of curtain calls
               and eventual pension, you went to the streets,
                    fields, and riverbanks, where with a glance

aside, the spell might break, the audience
          drift altogether away. Cursing superfluity
               you honed your acuity, furious to teach us
                    mesmerizing step and utterance

to the stretched limits of sufferance.
  You offered us, your steady troupe, grave
     occasions for dance: shell-shocked refugees
             and *Tzigane* deportees, Jehanne d'Arc's pyre.

But unexpectedly, cartwheeling from pestilence
          like a children's rosy-ring in a *danse macabre*
               we'd spin with spotlights the massive wheel

of our sixteen-meter tent frame, silver spokes
          whose apex under sailcloth was high overhead,
               its base planted solid on ordinary ground,

gravel, sand, or litter-strewn city weedlot,
          and two hundred eyes on your entrance.

Muse of dance

FOR EUTERPE

Huzzah, O huzzah — you voice
    of intelligible sanity. A woman
        bound by pacts and serene confidence

we can't touch, much less see; yet we hear
    clusters of notes forming chords, whose choice

means the force of life was never stronger
    as danger is beyond belief. Strange
        fruit, stained fools with bleached hoods

and sharpened pitchforks, or cops
    with lamps trained upon a face.
        Contemplate the opposite: bass drum
            broad as the grille of a Rolls Royce

and a tenor with butter in the bell.
    Ruminate in slow motion, inching
        through the melodious chain

of chambers with room for all
    comers: each hit, every noise
        doubling and tripling in time, band

comprised of gorgeous moving hands
    upon strings, valves, mallets, and keys,
        and ever over and under and now through
            the panoply circles a mind, in full voice.

When I was a child, with toys
    to stand in for the adult apparatus
        of saxophone, piano, and bass guitar,
            I would stride to a mirror in pantomime,

emulating as on stage the anticipatory joys
    of Jazz, which was love, which was ecstasy.
        I had no idea: What music could mean

to those who play (that's the word)
        not a game but a sinuous, agonized,
                sometimes jubilant wager on fate.
                        To a pubescent white kid with no ax

it seemed simple — music is a ploy, as
        cut of clothes or hairstyle or cash
                makes the man, so an instrument

is the ultimate accessory and prop.
        Imagine trysting the chanteuse,
                acrobat of emotion and femme fatale, who
                        to make 'em cry would kiss the boys . . .

But there was wonder beneath
        the superficial stupidity. I knew
                enough to listen, humbled and stilled,
                        and while life grew in pain, to rejoice

amid the shocking unalloyed
   complexity of our world, at war
        with concentration, bitterly suspicious
                of beauty. Your own songs melt schisms

among the elements, as sunlight will arise
        in torrential cascades, invisible energy
                reforming molecules, alchemizing atoms.

Your likeness in photographs, my only
        approximate image, yet engraved here
                inside me, motile in the fibers

from tapping foot to nodding chin,
        and sacred at the source is your voice.

For Calliope

Fierce political comrades, you two
       born on opposite sides of the rough Atlantic
           and carried by round-about routes to Boston,

battered harbor town where a revolution began,
       at first rhetorical, ultimately bloody. Who grew

up descendants of despising foes, just seven
       generations ago, now Allies. Both
           raised as daughters of such odd

mystical hybrids, rabbinical Anglican
       and semi-scholarly agitator. I see you
           standing fast in internecine intrigues: literary
               insurgents defying literal death, into

whose brittle membrane one has gone now,
       alone. What luck that I knew you, young
           as I was. In hopes of entering that double

magic circle, art & action, I sat enchained
       at the gates of Seabrook and Electric Boat,
           at the Gatling-gun range in Underhill. New

stripes of proficiency: charged "disorderly"
       for denouncing bombs that decimate
           whole neighborhoods. I would elevate
               you as pacifist *guérilleras,* with a view

to being comparably, virtuously black-and-blue.
           What are heroines? Fabulous mythical beasts,
               lettered and decorated, perfumed with sage.
                  Watching from elsewhere, often from afar,

those I admired appeared clear as dew
       and sublimely distilled, unencumbered
           by common burdens. As if — exhausted,

buoyed up in an instant when an image
        surges right into words; as if — alert
                for that chance, they'd simply unfold a sheet
                        and commence again. To scrawl, to fasten

phrases with syntactical screws.
        No doubt, in truth: you both knew
                great pain. Both bearers of sons.

Like the mother of Orpheus, bereft
        of belief, grieving his drowned head.
                With its legendary evergreen faith,
                        sour and sweet, the fruits of woody rue . . .

What gift will be granted to bless
        the novice, one seeking eloquence
                to warrant his elders' kindness?
                        Laureates surmounting pride through

honest work as teachers. Couriers, too
    responsive to spend days musing aloof.
                Two solitaries, resolved to participate
                        in the contradictory struggles of the age,

linking Guatemalans with Rosebud Lakotas
        and Roxbury squatters with L.A. gays.
                And recording, transcribing, all the while

stylus upon tablet, keystroke on linen rag.
        One I picture smiling from a window seat,
                sipping tumblered whisky. The other I see

behind mullioned glass as I ran past, globed lamp
        and angled brow. Compasses, reading true.

Muse of epic poetry

FOR URANIA

Ainigma, typographic cipher whose rhyme
  swivels steady but loose, eddy in a stream.
    You were actress then artist, made a poet

by catastrophe. Turned to words, in fact:
  when all's said and gone, quivering across time,

and voluminous. Look: picture as a painter would
  blazing huts in a circular village, colonial settlement
    constructed orderly as the solar system.

Flames gorge on roofs and walls, books
  beloved in exodus, the smoke-vomiting fire
    round which orbits the hierarchy of patriarch,
      matriarch, servant, and slave — a live

tableau inflected in the eyes of darker faces
  unseen beyond the edge of the trees.
    Colonists torched the forests to harvest

pot ash. *Artist, where's your plot?*
  A plot of ground, carbonous black.
    They dug from hillsides, mining lime

for metallurgy and to neutralize soils.
  Could paints convey the panoramic flux?
    But I fear I've melodramatized
      your difficulty, made a pantomime

in didactic prose. By contrast, sublime
  evaporation yields your lines — dexterous
    textured thinking grasped as moveable type.
      Not writer at a desk, but astronaut sprung by

photochemical combustion clear of the slime,
  projected over a globe whose reeling makes
    blurred and bleeding history, to make sense

now and then, astronomically perceived.
    Reader, so hesitant when unsure: terrified
        by new arrangements of familiar words
           or unable to see constellations turn, not

around the polestar but Southern Cross. Prime
    numbers are essential. Prime words
        granted weight, flint-edged arrowheads,

could be runes to mark the demise
    of theologies we blithely inherited.
        New equations, cerebral but tense
          with anguish, and spun on a dime

like a parabola distorted to reveal
    the flexed trajectory of a meteor
        through amnesias of darkened space
          and laid upon charts for maritime

navigation. Perhaps when it's seed-time
   the stars look arranged, dutifully arrayed,
     but at peak of drought in crop-blasting heat
      who could do otherwise but scorn

thoughts of pattern. Flung like stellar wild thyme
    upon the slopes, ripped and burst into bloom
        then abandoned as rubbish whole galaxies wide.

If words can do *justice*, can do damage
    to that boredom even language will induce,
        isn't it words knocked from mundane display,

now scrawled in radium with a half-life
    that instead of sliding down will climb?

Muse of cosmology

For Melpomene

What was tragic in fact was a call
    like the sirens' in the voice of one
        so sad: Grief, distrust. Genuine desire

undercut by remembered deceit.
    Whenever I think of her, if ever,

I'm re-immersed in pain. What
    unmitigated disaster. And what
        ridiculous misunderstandings, as I

followed her like a dog and became
    someone no friend could recognize.
        I made my moves, made eyes,
            made exceptions and provisions, as all

consolations made a huge difference.
    I'd inventory her sorrows and believe
        I was the remedy. Brother's suicide,

mother's addiction, raped by a comrade
    and betrayed by a husband ordained
        in a cult, whose grim tribunal

ruled her unfit as wife, hence
    their marriage untenable. Alas
        and alack, as tragedy it was classic.
            For more than a year, spring to fall

and back around again, an annual
    circuit of shame. Fawning. At my worst,
        as was she. Yet that year I'd plunged out
            from job and home to supposedly live by

my wits. Recall her shady rooms, in mutual
    (for the moment) calm. The *Barri Gràcia,*
        like an inner-city village or concrete glade

fountained and clock-towered, sunlit
      by tilting columns of fuel-scented light.
           Walking, eating; *lagostinos* and *vi tinto;*
                trailing the routes of Antoni Gaudí, monk

with pencil and transit whose cathedral
      accumulates endlessly as if built
           by mud-daubing wasps. And remember

the *Mercat de les Flors,* where another
      freak of intellect, Polish maestro Kantor,
           brought two hallucinatory shows to bear
                on our tiny stunned minds. If we'd at all

been ready, the weird vaudevillian mercy
      of those players would have lifted us clear
           into certainty then love. Despite the war's
                obscenity and outcome, the smoking pall —

they were comical as saltimbanques, like balls
      lofting wordplay above bowlers and shawls.
           The Artist Must Die: thus spake Tadeuz Kantor,
                but I could not surrender my pretensions

without a fight. So we fought. When mauled
      and reeling, no choice but to flee, at the last
           conceivable reprieve — struck and struck again.

Just words, but cruel as infidelity. Farewell
      to that dashing young man, "cool and fast,"
           so she'd hoped. Heart-set on being a savior,

engrossed in that image of our tragic Fate,
      I lost the crux of decency: we're lonely and small.

For Thalia

The stage constructed so a spotlight
    would pinpoint the solitary mouth: lips
        and teeth splayed in an opening stitched

in seamless black fabric that made a wall
    before Billie Whitelaw, hidden from sight

and bound in harness to bear the hour-long
    cyclone of words. Beckett's monologue
        cost her dearly in spasms and cramps,

myriad bruises, even blistered hands
    from gripping the rack. Yet she'd laugh
        to talk of *Not I,* how the maestro writhed
            at infelicities in delivery, if a pause went awry

as her voice let elide semi-colon or dash
    or mistook one for another, god forbid.
        I thought of you as I heard her speak,

though I've heard your voice almost
    never. Pen pal, foreign correspondent
        across years and miles, flight

of fancy gives you the mouth and mind
    of the unseen actress behind that screen.
        Known and adored by handwritten scores,
            a hundred airborne letters that might

just as well have gone astray as kites
    let swirl and glide at the outer stretch
        of twine sometimes disappear
            into invisible sky. In the mail

your frequent letter arrived with bright
    stamps and blurred postmark, as though
        funneled by miraculous chute or carried

quick by clever Hermes, if not Cupid. Here,
    see the box of epistles from two decades,
        a comedy of correspondences we did
            and didn't share in person, the hilarity

of mishaps and breakthroughs, days and nights
    recorded in scribbled running account
        one Scorpio to another, alter egos elusive

as a child's imagined elf. But, wait: could two
    confidantes so faithful as *doppelgängers*
        survive the climax of meeting face to face,
            or would both mirrors shatter at the sight,

collision of each parallel universe
    with its ineluctable match, its mate?
        No — more likely, at the instant
            of greeting, we'd split with glee in spite

of exaltation, our solemnity as slight
    as a streak of ink on unlined foolscap.
        In truth, I'm not sure we could tolerate
            the surprise: side by side, with spouse and child.

If I'd never learned that antique habit, to write
    down my thoughts and dreads and secret pursuits
        then seal them up in an envelope to fly by hook

or crook through slots and chambers, down
    conveyor belts and ramps, up elevators
        and into mailbags, I'd never have known

this spring of indispensable laughter, an ally
    inside me, friend fashioned of light.

Muse of comedy

For Clio

How many do you greet, Grace,
        with *Darling?* with *Sweetheart?*
           All your fledglings,

innumerable. I could not know
        the world as I do, careening in space,

without you — speaking as one
        of so many. That day on Wall Street,
           amassed in a blockade at the stock exchange.

You recall the stilt-walkers — three,
        with bass drum and tattering snares,
           who defied the actual gravity
                of our presence in that place,

waltzing towards an armored line
        of mounted police who forced
           three horses to charge fifty yards

of clattering pavement and crash
        squealing into the dancers' legs
           gruesome as the smell of mace

so they toppled upon the crowd
        and were lowered carefully down.
           There are those who hate us
                for merely believing. Your face

is inseparable from that phrase
        of Tranströmer's: *We have not*
           surrendered, but want peace. You
                live in multiple, overlapping realms,

disparate neighborhoods, a traveling case;
        I can't know all the others, but this one
           we share. Smarts Mountain commences

as though at the foot of your garden rows,
     rising in layers from your window sill,
         and from ours as well. This time of year
             bright ice crests the peak, startling

delicacy upon spruce and rock, a lace
     spun of frozen immaculate droplets,
         now acidic as vinegar. Yet gorgeous.

Chickadees stitch thin loops between
     feeder trees: almost needless to say,
         at moments one imagines a globe
            where the agony is effaced,

where the families are okay,
     the jobs are fine, international relations
         are steadily improving with the season,
            which has grown large, like a vase

filled with unimpeded light — *grace.*
     The maples and ash trees now childlike
         in their naked lack of leaves, with snow
            arriving wide and cold and clean to sight.

This storm is quiet as slumber, without trace
     of violence or strain. By evening, townsfolk
         assemblé not to protest or demonstrate

but as parishioners, approaching the church
     on the hilltop village green for vespers,
         a carol recital by candle-glow. While

a circle of friends will gather to say,
     Happy birthday. Dear Grace.

Muse of history

FOR POLYHYMNIA

Never had I known the rhyme or reason
        for that real resemblance between
                living woman and bowed instrument,

when we found a Bohemian *violoncello*
        in a shop off the route where the Prague police

regrouped and the wounded were solaced.
        Never had I understood the vocal art
                of drawing out from material things

the audible voice ingrained inside,
        as the fine, swirling lines in wood
                tell in melody a tale of tree and blade.
                        We were new to each other, seasoned

by mishaps and callused in romance.
        Yet tender, somehow — scribed with wry
                anticipation. And traveling east, at the onset

of Miranda's and Ferdinand's brave new world,
        euphoric to witness the collapsing Wall.
                In color, in tone, the cello was pleasing

and your phrasing with the strings
        a lucid contemplative breathing
                through the halls of boarding houses,
                        following the air currents to seize on

an attentive listener, who freed from
        knowing by way of words is released
                into knowledge more engulfing. J.S. Bach
                        made vast escapades with a solo cello

so seaworthy one travels dreams on
        these. In Casals' yellow bungalow in San Juan
                the suites play dawn till dusk in remembrance

of a Catalan refugee so arthritic at last,
    only practicing would unfasten the rack,
        as though Franco had hounded him clear
            to the islands but a portly, long-deceased

German cantor had bequeathed the means
    of taking refuge. Is it strange
        that I'm choosing this indirect path

to praise? Thinking of *you*. Your shape
    is actually very much like the cello's,
        while your voice is more beautiful,
            wending byways from second to season,

the difference between normal speech
    and flight-borne song truly slight, as breath
        fashions a different path from your lungs
            and spins curving in a glide that frees from

clinging gravity these syllables, to tease on
    invisible ropes, cords, and trapezes
        the air around us, vaulting the notes
            from your lips like acrobats or *coryphées*.

The vision is delicious, lowering like peace on
    a wounded mind, at the same time to beckon
        thoughts of being wrapped in you, our voices

and limbs, lying beside to intently confide
    in my consort, my cello, my wife. Bowed
        strings sigh like sonatas and moan

then commence again, and you sing as though
    any breath may shift to song as it leaves one.

Muse of sacred song

FOR ERATO

The surface well is shallow, but its water
      remains lucid — melodious to taste, as the tongue
            laps cold liquid pulsing up through the ground.

Our home is sited on old pasture above the well:
      long years of layered topsoil where fodder

grew and woolen lambs grazed; brief years
      since we came here to build upon its slope.
            Briefer still, the time passed since the little one

arrived home from the hospital, who delayed
      scarcely a fortnight before commencing to sing.
            Surely everyone feels this, of a child's voice.
                Her earliest vocalizing was a bright smatter

of accidentals and slanted grace notes,
      as she chased the shapes of gliding tones
            from her mouth through air sliding by

overhead. We listened and we gazed.
      By the second season, she could roll
            on Wellfleet's dunes, agile as an otter

and intent upon the spiraling sound
      of her mother's songs, or even my own,
            as her intensity of listening gave me
                every reason to sing, *alma pater*

and *alma mater,* anthems or ballads. As attar
      is fragrant so our sung refrains harmonized
            in her, it was plain to see. We gave her joy
                with songs, and pleasure was an avid teacher.

They tell us no substance is solid, that all matter
      constantly circulates with energized molecules
            which agitate in their infinitesimal haloes

even when rapt in apparent stillness. She
    demonstrates the principle, being all ways
        in motion. Swaddled babe then agile girl,
            she's devised to speak Girlish, language

with its own rules and lexicon (e.g. *waybo* ladder
    is the gadget on which a tired child climbs
        up the rungs each night to Dreamland) — so

we hear, as she's quick to explain, or quick
    to correct if we've misunderstood: *piptadoo*
        means "happy" and *noogatin* means "cheese."
            Sometimes I find it irresistible to quote her

when talk wends around to the brilliance
    of children, completely at home in worlds
        we can't imagine, realms of painted hue
            or commodious rhyme, life a full platter

of fanciful concoctions no reasonable doubter
    could confirm or deny. Listen as she sings,
        at her desk or playing dolls, for half an hour
            in the back seat of the car, complex medleys

of torch songs and hymns, torrid yet devout, her
    mama's jazz evergreens and Sunday's choral airs,
        What Shall I Give Him? Willow Weep for Me.

Wildest of all are the Christmas carols sung by
    barnyard beasts: her Dreamland Band
        has ducks with trumpets and drummer dogs,

fiddle-toting roosters with pounding hearts,
    and look! — in the middle, there's our daughter.

CODA: *Self-Portrait as Jehanne d'Arc*

And with that, I then
Began to hear
In the branches, in the leaves,
A lantern-lit, moth-begotten
Tolling of altered silence:
Holes in the universe, speaking.

So it was, will be —
Must have been. Every step I took
From the instant of laying down
A child's devotions,
Honey spoon and straw-gold blouse,
Was an ordinary step.
Riding out through the men in my leather breeches
— Every breath was only breath
Made of accident and purpose,
Fused moisture and air.

And everywhere we moved,
Every day — was hunger, the dry sponge.

Fire was near.
Fire was set there
To replace me
In my first unholy visions
And remained, fire in waiting.

God was anywhere
I put God. Side to side
In the ranks of soldiers
Or among the ghastly courtiers.
I could not divide
Myself from anything.
Snapped pennants that shine like blooded silk.
Muttering and chanting, the rocks
Wrapped in foam
In the stream below,

Inseparable from streaming flocks
In migrations above.

We cleave and are cleaved —
Annealed or annulled,
Baked in our hides by hammering sun
Or burst loose through openings
Jangling reflections of fire
Spear moment by moment
In the indivisible flesh.

They will offer me one hour
To recant. I will try
Again, to deny
Plume and blade, confess
All I've heard
Was the wind or wailing ewes,
Echoing of bells upon bells
Undulating with rapture;
Nourished, breast and brain,
By old bread soaked in wine.

Yet it's they who vanish
With the stroke. I can write
No name but my own.

I believe in the theater of bodies.
I believe we could live on the skin
Of a drum. Weighed down
Like a mule, I would carry you further.
With just enough water
To simply wet my tongue
I would sing the day longer, and spin

Into torchlight.

DWELLING

---

*If the desire for light is strong enough, and what
is desired is truly light, desire itself will produce
the light.*

Simone Weil

Home-made, home-made! But aren't we all?

Elizabeth Bishop

Consecration with Crow

1.
            We'd begun. You were mine.
In the summer of making our wedding vows
            we'd begun to build a house,
which would have no history but our own.
      Pasture pine and store-bought nails.

Where a dozer had crisscrossed the hillside
      sprung seeds went berserk
with clumped goldenrod and margaritas,
      black-eyed susans and the queen's frothy lace.

2.
The crow appeared
            suddenly, as if hatched
by inadvertent
            incantation.
Pinion feathers
            jagged as a fakir's
            tasseled vest.

Cinder-black shadow,
            not cast but embodied:
heard coming in fast
            before seen, then seen
askance at an eye's edge
            reversing direction
from a downward plunge
            to exact placement
of talons on the 2-by-6.

We've watched their flocks,
            plume-beaten velocity
            coasting treetops,
and languorous black tirades
where they congregate.
But this singular crow,

       so close: for the moment
claimed as ours,
       though no more ours
than a snake that sped
       unglimpsed across my ankle
in long grass, the hornet
       awakened in our sheets
as we lay down.
             Crow
traversing like a courier
       the wooded bowl below the site,
west from the Whitemans',
       north from the Eastmans',
pistoned flap and glide
     like a horn's overtones
     that linger.
See the torso between
       centrifugal wing span
whose down-stroke compresses
       the air below, creates vacuum above
which lifts — this is flight —
       pressure drop and updraft.

Arriving on your shoulder
       to snatch the pencil
from a pocket, brandished beak-wise
       like a crooked cigarillo.

So near: feathers upon spines,
       diametrical and multicolored
like oil on asphalt.
       Not fur, not scales, not skin:
The crow is nothing like us.
Widening its mouth so
       the bone-hard mouth pries out
a soothsayer's blackened Gaelic,
fluted diphthongs or fibrous

throat-worn creaks,
variable as reasoning,
        or shocking and abrupt
as raw exhalations of mood.

I cannot imagine this bird
        in an egg.
Big as a cat now,
        pointed at either end
like a double trowel,
        rocking beak and tail,
unpacking the nail can
like the derricks that preside
        over scrap yards.

3.
We who were migratory,
in transit even when resting down,
insatiable for elsewhere. We who
        encountered that household god,

        cracked and cockeyed
balladeer, vizier and anchorite,
        autochthonous novitiate
and sponsor of this
        clearing in the maples and pines:

We appear to have settled.
        Here as though forever.
This slope. This mix
        of hardwoods and soft.

With hammer and hand-saws
        (and what faith? what gall?)
    to build a house.
With pressing, fastening, sometimes adhering,
    to make a marriage.

Firewood

Poplar splits slippery clean once a maul finds its route through the log, massive and moist like hard cheese. White ash splits suddenly down vertical grain while sugar maple recoils sidewise across the saw cut, knotted whorl that spiraled as it grew. Every wood has its way against the blow, each its jacket and body: Black cherry, sheathed in cracked leather. Hornbeam in a hair shirt. White birch as flaky as the flesh of certain fish.

Not fond of chain saws, I'd rather pay for bucked stove-lengths or trade my time splitting the logs felled by a neighbor for the three cords we need.

Set eight or ten upright then take them at a cadence. Split steadily, without struggle. A six-pound maul-head is heavy enough, centrifugal force does your work. Handle raised like a banner pole, effectively resting, then let that steel wedge drop as if it were a whip lashed out and down, straight through the log to bury its edge in the block below. A second before the head strikes, imagine the wood fibers parting and opening, then watch this occur into four or five sections, like a spread blossom or quartered slices of fruit.

The heat embodied within, when put to flame — our many months of warmth, nourishing as the carrots and potatoes laid by in the cellar.

South Main Street, the Dorchester road, Route 10, Norford Lake Road, Route 122 on the Glover Heights, Union Village Road, then up Alger Brook Road on our spur knick-named Green Dolphin Street, now known as Blue Moon Road — through six moves in twelve years, I stacked wood in sheds, garages, dooryards, under eaves; stacked with parents, room-mates, girlfriends, house guests, and now my wife. At the home we've built ourselves the woodshed is sited beside a path from the driveway, rising rows of circular log-ends to the left and to your right the ground dropping off to garden, berry patch, and chicken-run then rising in tiers of conifers and hardwoods as we look east toward the Connecticut River, round-flanked serpent of fog dividing Vermont's layered green swathes from the further-off blue, New Hampshire's westernmost slopes and peaks.

Chickens scuffle and carouse underfoot despite the smack and rupture of the maul splintering logs. In early fall, stacking the last of our split wood we hear geese — far off, closer, then gone to Maryland's outstretched estuaries. One afternoon a goshawk on a pine branch surveyed our yard like a passing feudal lord, grand gray raptor as tall upon the bough as the distance between my elbow and upraised fingertips.

Worry — and work. Without that effort, hours and hours, felling and splitting, loading and hauling then stacking, come winter we'd freeze: stunned to the bone marrow, our lungs a crystallized lace. Winter forever coming on. Yet the black steel box of the woodstove will be the pulsing, radiant heart of our home.

Four Lullabies

. . . an antipodal, far-fetched creature, worthy of birth . . .
— Wallace Stevens

1. Cradle Song

Reapers and sowers, gleaners and drovers:
All go to sleep.
Plowers and fleecers: twelve o'clock mowers:
Go to sleep, to sleep.

As far, as far as we know.
As far as we know.

Elephant trainers: wallpaper hangers: corncob pipe-smoking porters:
Will all at the wave of a hat go to sleep.
Maplesap boilers: climbing rope coilers:
To sleep, before long — or gradually, to sleep.
Congressional pages: pundits and sages: acolytes and choir girls:
To sleep now, to sleep.

As far as we know.
As far as we know, we'll know.

Shopkeepers, goalkeepers, timekeepers, lighthouse-keepers:
At long last, to sleep.
Steeplejacks, lumberjacks, jack-hammerers, and apple-jacks:
To sleep, now — to sleep.

As far as we know, when we know;
as far as we know.

Deep as the chimney shaft
That passes your bed,
And wide as the rough black roof overhead:
Now to sleep, tiny child, now to sleep.

As far as we know.
As far as we know.

2. SUGARBUSH

Little heartbeat,
you make of bundled syllables a breath-long song,
quick and brief as condensation,
damp on my neck from your perch in the rucksack.

Two of us listening. Watching and listening:
you translate as *We too, we do*
the late winter call of the chickadee.

From a screened pail hanging halfway up the hillside
comes an arching blue hose,
slung by wires between trunks
to empty in an olive barrel at the road;

and buckets, each with its miniature roof,
mouths inverted like upended bells
that toll with the morning's thaw —
dripping sweetly, filling tremendously slowly.

We climb the slope at seven,
climb the eastern-facing sidehill
on snowshoes with a bucket-yoke.
The yoke's hooks dangle.

As we load on the liquid,
sap that forms droplets in the grooves of the taps
begins knelling in the emptied pails, tap-tapping
as on tin till the bottom is covered again,

and the smoke from three houses lifts in gray-green lianas,
rolls from chimney caps down roofs
that seem lowered with the weight and height of whiteness
to touch with their eaves the mounds beneath.

As you sleep, little minstrel, it will be
mid-morning in your dream, propped in the backpack
at the cleft of two maples.

Eyes closed. Ears beneath a wool cap, covered.
Listening but not watching

till a woodpecker strikes the popple trunk
with the force of its beak through bark

and you grin.

3. To the Winds

The giraffe and the weathercock
Wind from the south and wind from the east
Stretch their necks toward the lark
Wind from the north and wind from the west

Each of these lives near the sky
Wind from the south and wind from the east
As high as the swallows are high
Wind from the north and wind from the west

And the swallow pirouettes like a whirligig
Wind from the south and wind from the east
In summer above the weathercocks
Wind from the north and wind from the west

The swallow's signature is a looping graph
Wind from the south and wind from the east
All winter long round the necks of giraffes
Wind from the north and wind from the west

after Robert Desnos

(Paris, 1900 — Terezín transit camp, 1945)

4. Lullaby with Benjamin Schwartz

Pressed brow to the evening's ceiling
which almost presses back,
yielding to thought.
Draw down the bottle to its froth,
and that's done. So's the day.
And the lights ring lightly on breeze,
tinkling like spoons in soapy bowls,
as the bells of a flock on small hooves
go home across the hill.

Give us simply the frayed edge
of last night's dream
to follow back in, threaded by fingers
as hands will, with a bolt of fabric.
Give us a few inches of wick to ignite
as darkness thickens.
Give us saturation and sleep.

Enough of today,
said Benjamin Schwartz
     every night at eleven,
in a funny white house no longer white
     or no longer still there.
Now as far away as twenty years,
     like so I still remember him,
        even so, you will too.

Through the windows
     praying owls are chanting over mice.

Give us sleep, with saturation.
Terrible height and breadth and depth,
     but you in your pocket of linens
        have no reason to wake
until daylight.

DEVOTIONAL

Now we live our life
        upon the marriage breadth —
stripped of outer bark,
sawed and planed lengthwise
        then jointed in dovetails, and
        hand-polished,
            confiding as never before
with body-sundering confidence;
        the sealed secrecy of youth
        opened wide
to leave any light glean
on its grain.

     •

One, another. And we
        multiplied: how can this
      irreducible child
      with her speed and gaiety
be? Flesh and blood
        exponential in its blue-eyed force,
      a genetic bouquet.
A blur as she grows.

Overhearing overhead
      the ripple of steps upon floorboards
        as we rest arm in arm,
        sharing a chair.
Upstairs in the room where we made her,
         she plays *This Old Man* with sticks
on lids from emptied jars.

     •

    Hear one plea
when I say, let each of us three
        live to be old.

Willingly at last would I
        place a faith in vacant air,
obediently strung to the buoyant invisible
              we stride beneath,
                      glad-footed trio of marionettes.

     •

Because simply
         arranging our daughter's bedclothes, with a tug
               on the linen releasing
perfume of perspiration and chamomile soap
                   will set off such trembling
             in dissolved morning light;
         then folding your clothes
just laundered, dried by the wood stove —

                  the sense of smell is ravenous
        as you know, for these
              blessed scents of kin:
        the cotton jersey you work in,
            or stockings for nights of singing
                translucent as fragrance,
jade dress and cream-colored blouse,
        mine to hold as I fold them.

     •

        If I might be
so bold,
          if I may —
Give us these days.

IN SEASON

If the world were just, it would suffice to build a house.

Arthur Schopenhauer

Not that I want to be a god or a hero.
Just to change into a tree, grow for ages, not hurt anyone.

Czeslaw Milosz

NEW YEAR'S EVE

Girlish still, in mildness and spark,
surviving in a skeleton
fragile as an armature of reeds.

Rubber-treaded soles
should soften the shock
of my arrival, but she startled up

from the gurney
and the morphine,
eyes wide across acres of hours:

*I will never go home. My house
was sold* — while droplets condensed
on the murky sacs of an IV rack.

As no family was near,
I sat with her for the night shift,
evening to sunrise.

They said, "Oxygen-starved,
she's unlikely to eat." She said
Air is unprized ease —

in the margins of a magazine
I transcribed what I heard.
So fitful in sleep

yet lifting to a rinsing lucidity
— *Does it frighten you to go
before you've understood?*

Note the rise and fall,
every breath released
like a sigh. In advance,

our unspoken goodbye.
— *Pretty boat . . . What boat is this?*
Now a row of faces. All so small.

Later when I had gone
they completed her chart.
Empty johnny and wrist tag.

This was New Year's Day.
Vague sun pressed through mist
thin as watered milk.

First dawn in a century
to find her

nowhere on earth.

Double-Take

The double glance, swiveling chin and forehead
as her face with those lips, yes lips, came around my way
to gaze back over a leather-jacketed shoulder.

Memorable as one eyelash, resting on the back of a hand.

Rarely do I sense myself seen as a man anymore, a man,
but instead as passerby, middle-aged, middle-browed.

Treachery in the thought, with instant misgivings —
but what rapid awakening in synapses and nerves
is criminal, if seen through? I see through

the long-steeped hunger, and let that be, subsiding.

Like a quarter cup of milk, the winter's moon.

INQUEST, BY HAND

Eastertide

The body prone — almost flat
on its back, but appearing torqued
crosswise to the spine

to fit the truncated box.
If not for his face, with cosmetics
made smooth as wax,

one might say sound asleep, but he's
beyond sound, swathed in the *huzz*
of refrigerated blooms.

Crescents of reflected light
behind lids they closed
part-way.

A coroner would know
a human hand could be
so cold:

suddenly alone with the body in state,
for no reason *per se* I took
that hand in mine

and held on. Embalmed, the thing was like
a metal knob in sub-frozen December,
each molecule of warmth

sucked away as what I clasped
took my pulse and flung it
to ground, zeroed at root.

As cold moved upward via the blood
in my arm, I was waiting
— for what?

Incubus and succubus, no longer incarnadine,
one body above and the other beneath.
A mystic will warn

your *pneuma* can be squandered,
stolen by a reckless touch.
        But I held on.

Enormous deletion, smothered in propane
while lacing his boots. The dead boy's hand
larger than my own,

rimed with calluses from pencils and pliers,
a hand I never grasped alive
with *Salut — Ça va?*

My fingers, palm, and forearm gone numb.
Waiting for a sign from within or without,
 in his tongue or mine.

Instead *Hush* went the ventilators, sucked wind
from below, chilling us to stillness.
        The cadaver was quiet.

BIRD SONG

As doves do seem to moan,
as the amusing uplift of a warbler
flutters into tune
and a grosbeak slides glissandos
through the ash tree's come-lately buds

pillow talk *chez nous*
mating calls, *chez eux*

Smooth — you,
every part of you I touch
with open hand,
thin fabric between
thee and me.
You asked if I'd ever
         used *caress*
when writing. If not yet —

Alas, interrupted
(not this time by our child, who's away)
we catapult from bed
and run outside to shout off
a sapsucker
hammering holes
beneath the eave.

Too late to go back to bed,
yet let's stall briefly
before giving in
to the day's duress —

Could you call this couch
a love seat? Yes.

So long beyond reach,
shorted-out
by anxiety and exhaustion,

these strained nerves
revive, intertwined:

What a jolly surprise
to coincide
with daybreak, accompanied
in bird song.

OUT-OF-DOORS

after René Char

A BIRD . . .

A bird sings on a wire
Of this common life, from blossom to earth.
By our hell delighted.

Then the wind begins to suffer
And the stars consider.

Ah dear fools, to fall
So far into bottomless fate!

THE ROOM IN OPEN AIR

Like the ring-dove's song when the downpour is at hand —
    air powdered in rain, the sunlight ghostly — I wake
    washed clean, I melt in rising; I gather the vintage of a
        newborn sky.

Alongside against you, pressing your liberty. I am a lump of earth
    reabsorbing its flower.

Is there a carved throat more radiant than yours? To ask is to die.

Your sigh's wing lays a downy quilt on the leaves. In one draught
    my love encloses your fruit, drinks it down.

I'm in the grace of your gaze, which my darkness surrounds in joy.

How lovely the cry that yields me your silence!

WIRE

The child said
our line is empty, no
dial tone, no hum

though we'd spoken to you
over the river
not minutes ago,

laugh that thumped
a diaphragm beneath
the ear piece

as shuttled magnets
interrupt
an electron stream

to approximate
speech

.

With wind coming on hard
in chilly summer woods, thighs
gashed through pants by berry wands

I follow the phone line
in its smooth black rind
looping without poles

over branch stubs or dragging
low through leaf wrack
a mile from the junction box;

touch disconnected leads
with electrodes on a multi-meter
set for ohms

seeking *infinity*
which I find; then
with the house side re-joined,

test for *continuity* —

not found; then eventually see
the storm-split cherry tree
that severed the wire

      •

Slice the cable sheath
unwrap those shining threads
in its core to re-entwine

long ago, the metal called Cyprian

a pair of filaments
thin as a baby's hair
yet miles in length

dug from slopes above town,
our old Elizabeth Mine's yield
perpetually re-employed,
smelters to rollers to wire —
when pure, dazzling
in conductivity

through my fingers
the current resumes
low-voltage, textured

like velvet in the ear,
and who's at the far end,
as here

we hear the scrambling chime?
It's you, your voice
in the receiver

transfigured, complete.

Hex

on a stolen ladder

A ladder leaned at a roadside ash tree
beneath a drooping black wire
so any passerby could see
my phone-line repair was half done.
Whoever you are,

may fingers pinch and knuckles scrape
each time you slide the extension sections.
May the pet ferret in your jacket pocket
(yes, I imagine that, there)
startle at the aluminum-rattle on the roof rack
and grip your nipple with its eye teeth.

May you poke open with the uprights
in the rotten soffit under an eave
a tumbling nest of skewer-tailed bees,

and two stories high
to paint gable trim or prune a limb
may your saw snag,
your bucket dump oily green stain
or your bootsoles slip
so your chin smacks each rung
all the way down
while a stripe gets tattooed groin to brow,
rope-burned by the lifter cord.

May your fuel-filter cake and your carburetor spew gas

through the heater vents
and your afternoon beer evaporate from unopened cans.

My wife would say in this life we'd better not curse,
and shouldn't waste words. She'd remind me
the Pope forgave even a would-be assassin.

Sooner would I *plead* than *damn*
(I'd rather have our ladder back)
but shouldn't I be satisfied
if back-diving from the ladder struck by lightning
you survived
with only one leg broken
in a quarter-acre patch of ripened poison ivy?

Autumn Equinox

The morning glories
continue knowing
nothing,

but such a caprice,
that lavish clambering toward
— what? Only sunlight.
For this the open, every day.

The grief
I feel can't be
described.

In moonlight broad
as the sprawled land we look across
the blossoms are closed
like miniature umbrellas,
our clothes on the line
colorless yet bright
beneath a white platter of mercury

that orbits a world
where our dear ones
die.

These nights we hear transports
from the airbase upstate.
These days I hear fighter jets
going east
at ungodly speeds.

The morning glories are
— what colors?
"Blue as our girl's eyes," or bluer.
Tinted rose, as wishful thinking is said to be.
Wrinkled slightly like crepe paper
with white centers,

on avid green vines that climb
whatever we do

defying all
but
the killing frost.

UNMEMORIZED MAN

> *Life leaves us habits in place of happiness . . .*
> *Where is the golden certainty of my youth?*
>
> Tchaikovsky's *Onegin*

Old man, not so old
but with beard twigged and thready as a nest
and his chest like a slack-bellied steer's.
Impressive even now, six foot five,
one who'd give you pause.
Not my own but my wife's
addle-pated uncle, name of Ron
— as he says: *Ron Quixote,*
Man of Dementia. Our tattered knight.

He loves recitals and symphonies
as he's listening, but later . . . ?
Take him to dinner and a show,
when you drop him off he'll know,
but by dawn or next noon
he can't recall. *What? Where? With you?*

As he wanted his own car
(his *own* — for how long?)
I showed him the way in mine,
from one town to the next, belayed
on lit lines from headlights,
and for every few seconds looking forward
I'd peer back through my mirror to see
his hands, white-knuckled on the steering wheel,
and thrusting face, eyes held fast on my tail-lamps.

He adored the opera, and as we
descended the stairs, each with an arm
over the other one's shoulders, he said
What do they see, Coupla gay guys, yah?
Out on the town. Or father and son.

A vast laugh tipped his girth,
and rain swept over us, brittle curtain
drawn across trees and old gray fields.

But: *Where's my car parked?* Then, *Which car?*
and *What road will take me home?*
Which house? What life, with which wife?

And he groaned, *I've got no rearview mirror.*
This is no joke.

Home, we were only driving home,
five miles of fog-smeared blackness,
the mass of moisture not presence or substance
but something scraped from view,
the vacuum beyond almost seen.
Only twenty years between us, and twenty feet,
while the eight tires of our two battered jalopies
whipped circles of spray like dories in swells
through a sunken, saturated place

near the cattail marsh
where a friend passed in thick mist thirty years ago
and was suddenly surrounded
by a herd of horses he had to swerve between,
and one kicked out a taillight.
Not even there, I only heard the story
but I hear a hoof crack and the shattering lens,
one of countless memories: *carried how? From where?*

Him or me, who is who, I believe
I'm sure I know who's in the lead,
I'm in front glancing back.
My eyes in this storm, tiny lenses for a mind
not unlike a sleet-smeared, night-struck windshield
in a car with no view to the rear, driven by a man
without memory of what's behind.

Imagine how he feels: Mouse-nest of riffraff
in the inner ear; sheaves of flies' wings
under eyelids, which obscures his gaze,
and belly enlarging like a balloon pumped ever more —

But that's so fanciful. In truth, his vantage is bland.
Waking to coffee and toast. Then coffee, toast, and cold cuts.
Later gin and toast, or canned soup (a burner left on for hours),
or many nights, a carton of some fried thing. With pie.

Fugue-like, these wiper blades' staggered sweep.
The radio plays an aria from the opera we saw.
Cascades of static tumble across the broadcast like sand
circling the tight ligature of an hour glass . . . skidding down . . .

From where? Toward where?

DAUGHTER

When older herself
with hair streaked white
and sagging a little, below

will she say of me
"He was well known," "He was well-to-do"?
(not likely)

"He knew what he wanted . . ." ?
"He was sometimes at loose ends" ?
Or, if I'm lucky,

"He drove slowly enough
to miss swallowtails and frogs."

"He read to me
        Little Women, Anna Karenina,
        Mrs. Dalloway and *Beloved.*"

"He baked the family's bread."

Nativity Pageant

And a child shall lead them.

Isaiah

I.

Refugees, townsfolk, penitents and thieves
shuffle in orbit around the fulcrum
of an invisible cradle.

No firmament above. No celestial harmonies,
but cowbells, rattle of snares,
tuneless sighs on clay ocarinas
while an antiquated eight-year-old
stoops past with pole and birdcage,
as burlapped twins haul a hamper,
and one young woman light on her feet
lifts a reed-woven fan for shade.

With brief greetings they cross
shoulder to shoulder, hand on hand:
their common currency
a certain dread.

II.

Every head of household
must return with wife and offspring
to his place of birth
to be counted and taxed.

Their understanding
bears
no consequence. They have
no idea
what arises in time.

Yet the brightest image imaginable
is the illuminated face
of a child Madonna —
her cloak cerulean, her grange
a lean-to rigged in canvas and twine,

knobbed saplings with straw underneath.
The flock is a set of wooly bags that swing
like marionettes from the shepherds' fists,
            our daughter among them,
and several donkeys and calves,
swathed broomsticks with bobbing heads.

III.
Cosmos wide
as a wing-spanned mind
yet thin as the hymnal's page.
In a basin appears the swaddled Christ.

Unstained glass in the congregational panes,
unprismed glare as a late-day sun
streams sideways
through winter's brittle grains.

Devoid of faith, yet I hear
glazed feathers layered on little racks,
skirted gowns lifted by tiny hands
when angels climb steps to the altar-side

where firs spread shadowed boughs
below a candelabra,
my wife's piano playing the tonics
with counter-pointed bells

like buoys on a tide
to greet the dark clarinets
of three stilted kings
striding up the center aisle.

Whatever has occurred, intangibly —
what lyrical commencing toward
        what gruesome end —

with what certainty?
The young proclaimer has a voice
               that could be heard
at the steeple's height:

O season of Light

For the children, an ever-enlarging grace;
but for the woman and man
who know what penance is due?
Massacre of the innocents:

Herod's ghastly promenade
is a horn-crowned, spear-flanked teenaged boy
proceeding across the floorboards
with yards of crimson silk

pooling from each ankle,
glistening hallucination
lit by floodlamps.

IV.
Refused protection in any city or town.
Reviled as outcasts from beyond.
One family more,
with three mouths to feed.

Who's heard word of freedom land,
          across the river's shore?
These players have glimpsed their Canaan.

Though dark is pressing down
see what lasts —
the even-handed decency of daylight.

for

the musicians and bread-bakers

and for

Duncan Nichols,
Janey McCafferty, Michael Johnston,
Rebecca Bailey and Ann Aspell

Certain poems have special dedications: "Land Alone," Alan Weisman. "War Zone," Kimiko Hahn. "On Green Dolphin Street," Sydney Lea. "Self-Portrait as Jehanne d'Arc," Patti Smith. "Firewood," Ben Bradley and Tii McLane. "New Years Eve," Anne Slade Frey (1900–1992). "Inquest, By Hand," Laure-Anne Bosselaar. "Autumn Equinox," Anneli Frykberg (who died in 2002) and Martin Osterland (1937–2000). And "Nativity Pageant" is for two radical pastors: William Sloane Coffin (1924–2006), whose parish always had room for doubters, and Garret Keizer, whose essays put my conscience to ice and fire, like tempering a blade. "Devotional" is for Rebecca and Lillian, of course, but appears here with a thank you to Christopher Merrill, celebrant of psalms.

I thank the editors of the following periodicals, in whose pages some of these poems appeared, often in different versions: *Blue Buildings* (M. R. Doty), *The Harbor Review* (Denise Levertov), *Ironwood* (Michael Cuddihy), *Northern Woodlands* (Stephen Long and Virginia Barlow), *Poetry International* (Fred Moramarco), *Orion* (Christopher Merrill), *Rivendell* (Sebastian Matthews), *The Strafford News* (Kate Linehan), and *The Valley News* (Kathryn Stearns); and the internet literary sites *In Posse Review* (Ilya Kaminsky) and *Poetryfish* (Marv Klassen-Landis and Phil Singer). Other poems were featured on Garrison Keillor's radio program "The Writer's Almanac" and in a musical setting by composer Paul Carey; in the anthologies *Never Before: Poems About First Experiences* (Laure-Anne Bosselaar, editor; Four Way Books, 2005), *Good Poems* (Garrison Keillor, editor; Viking Penguin, 2002), *The Breath of Parted Lips, Volume II* (Sydney Lea, editor; CavanKerry, 2004), *Best Spiritual Writing 2000* (Philip Zaleski, editor; HarperCollins, 2000), *Heartbeat of New England: Contemporary Nature Poetry* (James Fowler, editor; Tiger Moon, 2000), and *Articulations: The Body and Illness in Poetry* (John Mukand, editor; Iowa University Press, 1995); and in a chapbook, *One Another* (Chapiteau Press, 1999).

Publishing a first book in my fifties, I have many gratitudes. Ilya Kaminsky and Mariela Griffor, what a pleasure to know you. For time and room to concentrate, thank you to Robin Jaccaci and your marvelous house and to Gary Clark and your confreres at the Vermont Studio Center. I'm so grateful to my parents Imy and Ned and my siblings Dan and Sally and your families, and to my teachers, especially Ellen Bryant Voigt, Richard Corum, and Sydney Lea as well as the original muses. For camaraderie and audaciously good examples, I thank troupes of players in Bread & Puppet, The Expanding Secret Company, Les Montreurs d'Images, Signal & Noise, Duncan Nichols's merry crew, and Flock Dance Troupe. Profound thanks to hardworking colleagues and Trustees at The Frost Place and beloved neighbors at Blue Moon Cooperative. And for stoking this writer's hearth on the coldest nights and days, I send love and thanks to friends and relations who encouraged me, responded to poems, invited me to give readings, or hired me for jobs. You've made a difference.